This book bel

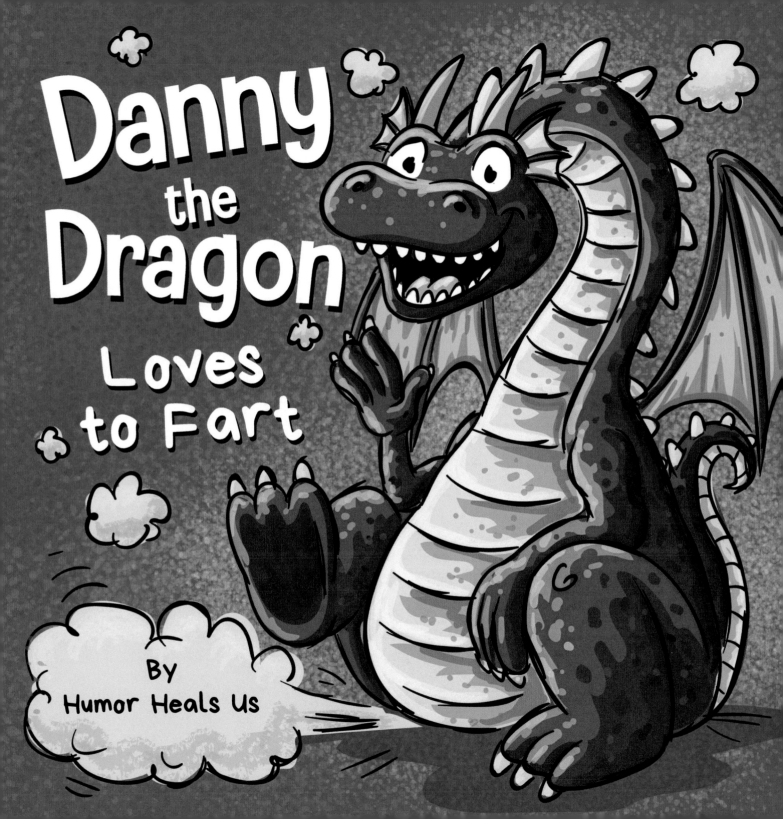

He loved to fly up, up, up,
In between the clouds as they would part,
But Danny's favorite thing to do
Was to propel himself with **FARTS**!

He'd toot his way through the sky,
Passing gas while flying past the birds.
His air bagels were some of the loudest
That anyone had ever heard.

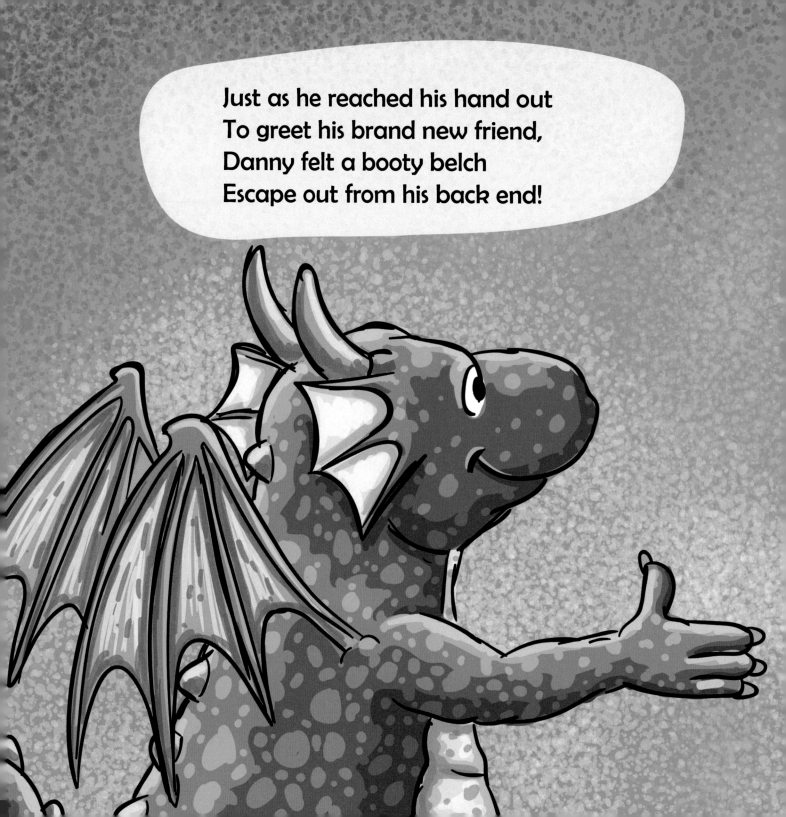

HEY, what was that sound
Coming from down the road?"
It was coming from a dragon named Francis,
As Danny waved and let his pooter explode.

Danny wished he wasn't the only one,
Passing gas and dropping fart bombs.
He wished the other dragons
Would join him in a butt bazooka song.

And THEN, all of a sudden,
He heard a little squeak.
Tim started blushing, his cheeks turned red,
As he opened his mouth to speak.

He reminded Tim and Francis
Passing gas is actually a good thing.
It's healthy (even when it's smelly),
Despite the stink they bring.

So the next time you feel you need to air whistle,
Whether it sneaks out quiet or loud,
Think of Danny the Dragon,
And just know you're making him proud!

Visit us at humorhealsus.com for book sets and toy box sets soon!

@humorhealsus     @humorhealsus